Rose Petal Poems-
Tales of Life and Love

Poetry can be a glimpse into a soul
that you might otherwise never know.

.......Eddie D. Wilcoxen

CTK PUBLISHING

Or write to: CTK Publishing,
              712 East Walker Street,
              Altus, Oklahoma 73521

Visit www.eddiestuff.com
for information on other books and projects.
Schedule an appearance or email comments:
eddie@eddiestuff.com
or write to:
> *Eddie Wilcoxen*
> *712 East Walker Street*
> *Altus, Ok 73521*
> *Phone 580-471-9733*

Photographs by Eddie D. Wilcoxen
Taken at Wilcoxen Gardens in Altus, Oklahoma.

LIBRARY OF CONGRESS CATALOGING-IN-PUBLICATION DATA
ISBN 978-1-934483-14-5
PRINTED IN THE UNITED STATES OF AMERICA - FIRST EDITION

CTK PUBLISHING

Introduction

Well, here we are at book number lucky eleven! Who can believe it? It is far beyond anything I envisioned when I was writing <u>Reflections of a Wandering Mind.</u>

I have really enjoyed most every step of this poet's journey, and I wouldn't have done it without you. Thank you for all the support and encouragement.

In this book I've pulled back the curtain to reveal that tender side that so many of us hide away from the outer world. Welcome to <u>Rose Petal Poems - Tales of Life and Love.</u> I've found that for me the key is poetry. It takes me to places that are normally private, then gives me a vehicle for sharing. I find it easier to write the words and then read them than it is to just say them in the first place.

Passion, romance, betrayal, death, whimsy - all these are the heady topics of <u>Rose Petal Poems.</u> Hopefully, something here will speak to the romance in your soul - will nurture those tender feelings that seem to attune us a little better to life and love.

....Eddie D. Wilcoxen

CONTENTS

For those with romance in their soul,
Who believe in things they cannot know,

For those who feel the power within,
A strength beyond muscle, blood and skin,

For those who know love's strength,
Who sense its breadth and depth and length,

I dedicate this book to you.
May you find love in all you do!

..............Eddie D. Wilcoxen

Rose Petal Poems-
Tales of Life and Love

by
Eddie D. Wilcoxen

Entry into the Forest Glen, Wilcoxen Gardens, Altus OK   Photo by E. Wilcoxen

Enter In

Enter in the garden gate.
You're welcome here, my love.

Walk with me this garden path.
Share blessings from above.

Enter in this garden gate,
Portal to worlds beyond,

Because hand in hand we're more.
Gentle embrace, superhero strong!

Come with me through this gate.
Live in soft enchantment.

Dwell with me where magic grows,
Home of the fairies great encampment.

Enter in this garden gate,
We'll stroll the rose lined trail.

Enter in, with me, my love,
Find shelter from the world's travail.

For Lovers Everywhere

Oh, Danny boy, the pipers are all gone,
And Romeo and Juliet -
They will never see the dawn.

Marc Antony and Cleopatra fell to sword and bite.
Only we are left
To speak for love tonight!

What can we say, except life is fleet,
But the taste of love
Is oh, so sweet!

Good-bye to Jack and Jackie in Camelot's mighty hall.
Farewell to Don Juan
Whose search for love took all.

Gone King Edward, woman rather than throne,
And Lancelot and Guinevere
With the only love they'd known.

Great love, passion pure, burned upon the pyre!
And only you and I are left
To feel love's fierce desire.

For lovers everywhere, it must be you and me.
So hold me dear, and kiss me sweet.
Just we two hold the key!

Science of Love

Love! Nothing more than chemicals,
So the scientists say.

Nothing to get excited about -
Men and women are just made that way.

It is the hormones and the genes;
It's a chemical reaction.

Ah, yes, science can explain it all,
This giddy way we're actin'!

But science never felt heart so light,
Nor contentment run so deep.

Science doesn't know the gentle touch -
Can't hear the whisper sweet.

So, let the slide rules rule!
Let the test tubes clatter!

Heart to heart, hand in hand,
Is all that will ever really matter!

Paper Lantern, Paper Moon

Paper lantern, paper moon,
Paper stars dispel the gloom

And cast the most romantic glow
On those gathered down below.

Paper lantern by the sea,
Paper moon high in a tree -

Each spell romance,
At least to me.

Softer light and loving words -
Whispers in the night – only we heard.

Beneath the glowing paper light
We danced away an enchanted night.

In the breeze the gentle sway
Of paper lanterns led the way

Across the floor and into the night,
Where in love's embrace we held tight.

Paper lantern, paper moon,
Bless your light and see you soon.

Shine on, shine on, for lovers!
Cast your glow in pastel colors.

Pink, blue, and green - a lovely sight -
Create your magic in the night.

For lovers will always heed
The beauty of the light you weave,

And suspending reality for just a while,
Will see paper moons and start to smile!

Wilcoxen Gardens, Altus OK   Photo by E. Wilcoxen

Ruby Beach

The battered land has retreated,
Leaving pillars of rock.
They stand alone in blue Pacific water,
Sheltering the seabird flocks.

Travel down, down to the water,
Over giant logs bleached white.
Wherever ocean meets land in Washington,
It's a common sight.

Like's God's pickup sticks,
They lie in tangled heaps,
Intricately intertwined here in the sand,
Cast up from the deep,

By the fury of the sea!
Ahh, but that was another day.
The sun shines clear and warm
And the wind has naught to say.

So, we wander Ruby Beach,
And marvel at the ebbing tide.
Not the least of miracles,
This woman at my side.

Hand in hand we sit,
And quietly as one,
We listen to the ocean roar
Its tale of love that's never done.

Rose Petal Poem

Falling
    Words.
        Pretty,
But far less than the whole.

Soft words.
Scattered across the page -
The searching never gets old.

It's a rose petal poem,
A lovers tome,
That cannot reach its mark.

Just another rose petal poem,
Not quite right,
Yet somehow, still, it touches your heart!

Angel Wings

I hear your gently beating heart,
The faint stir of angel wings.
Everything is right with all the world,
You're in my arms again!

Softly I enfold you,
Your lips are pressed to mine.
I feel the Heavens pouring out
Our true love's flowing wine.

I know that this one moment
Will fade with passing time,
But the memory of our love, dear,
Is etched deep upon my mind.

That sweet thought of us together
Will keep and guide us as we go
Through the trials and tribulations
Of this old world below!

Then someday, we'll be forever
In Heaven's old sweet by and by.
I know we will rush together
To see the love light in our eyes!

Let the angels sing a chorus!
Their sweet voices loud will ring!
Then we'll always be together
And never want for anything!

I hear your gently beating heart,
The faint stir of angel wings.
Everything is right with all the world,
You're in my arms again!

Angel Statue, Wilcoxen Gardens, Altus OK   Photo by E. Wilcoxen

Remembered Love

Remembered love,
A cup of bitter sweet.
Soft sighs and lonely tears
Fill the empty space
Bereft of passion's heat.

It seems all was right
When you were mine.
But truth to tell,
It's more impression
Than remembered lines.

Through rose colored glasses,
I'm looking at the past,
And wondering why
Something so wonderful
Just did not last.

Remembrance

The tides of passion rise.
The moon is full and high,
Rolling languidly across a darkened sky,

As I wait for you, my love.

Bodies collide, and with bated breath
Fall together in the wooded steppe,
Living in the moment of the little death,

And I want for you, my love.

The years have dimmed the eye,
Events swiftly flowing by.
Still, I recall your every sigh.

Yes, I remember you, my love.

Searching Heart

The heart is a lonely hunter,
Single and solitary in its search.
They say it wanders random -
No master plan does its name besmirch.

With only rhymes, not reason,
It lurches here and there,
Always searching for another heart
With everything to share.

Long years may go in the telling,
Or strike like lightning from above.
The quest for a kindred soul
Is the sacred search for love.

And one heart can only seek one heart,
There is no other way.
The heart is a lonely hunter.
Wish him luck as he brings his prey to bay!

Joan's Rose

This red rose speaks of passion
And truth,
The first blush of youth –
And you.

This red rose knows the secrets
Of private things,
And wedding rings,
And yes, it's true,

This red rose carries
The beauty of love,
And blessings from above,
From my heart straight to you!

Black Eyed Susans in Wilcoxen Gardens, Altus OK   Photo by E. Wilcoxen

Ever New

I see flowers everywhere
Rolling round the garden's bend!

Yellow faces shining -
I look, then look again.

So many times I've seen them,
Yet the sight is ever new -

Much like the way I feel, my dear,
Each time I look at you!

On March 28, 2011 NASA's Swift satellite discovered a gamma ray burst unlike any known before. Research later identified it as the sound of a "shredded" star disappearing into a black hole.

…..Eddie D. Wilcoxen

Shredded

It's the last scream of a shredded star,
Going down that old black hole -
Much like the sound of lonely,
From my own shredded soul!

It truly is a gamma burst,
But then it fades away to nothing -
A lot like the end of love
When you don't see it coming.

The dying star lingers at the edge,
Heats, and then suddenly is gone -
Screaming like my heart!
God! How long does this go on?

Snake Oil and Candy Kisses

All that Hollywood handsome
And honeyed tongue -

Remember those men
From back when you were young?

The ones who promised everything
And meant not a single line?

The ones keeping score,
Leaving you to fret and pine?

They never cared for you,
Only for the chase.

You were just a conquest,
Forgotten in their haste,

Their need to be off in search
Of new and fresher blisses.

Too late you learned that they were
Just snake oil and candy kisses!

Carousel

Ahh, that carousel,
Where the pretty horses play!

Cotton candy smells,
Warm summer days.

Peals of laughter, squeals of delight,
Round and round!

Calliope pumping,
Innocence found.

It was a small city park,
A lifetime ago,

When the world was new
And there was nothing
I did not know!

Around Again

All the animals go up and down,
Round and round, on the carousel.

Pretty painted horses;
I remember well!

The calliope belts out its tune
Of cotton candy, smiles, and laughter.

As I seize hold of that long lost pole
I find the refuge that I'm after.

Seeds of Optimism

All the flowers that will ever be
Are in the seeds of this one day,
As every great deed that is yet to be
Will grow from yesterday.

The future is born of the past,
The past from days gone by.
We stand upon the shoulders of giants
As we reach into the sky!

Sometimes the world so quickly changes,
It seems almost surreal,
But at the core there are values still
That will keep it true and real.

Honesty, courtesy, gentleness, and faith -
These seeds will grow a mighty crop!
So plant them deep, and tend them well.
Believe and never stop!

Then, in a day that's yet to come,
We'll see a brighter future flower,
As our hopes and dreams grow and blossom,
To fill all of mankind's bower!

Moon Dance

"Wake up, wake up!" the full moon cried.
"It's time for dance and song!
Get up, get up! Get moving!
You cannot tarry long!"

So from my bed I tumbled
And rushed to greet the night,
Illuminated by the smiling moon
With silver flowing light!

The lightning bugs were calling
To glow worms down below,
While the water danced and tumbled -
Now that's a song I know!

So we spun like whirling dervishes
Out into the light.
Hand in hand we danced and laughed
Deep into the night.

Until, at last, in weary exhaustion,
Upon a rock, we came to rest,
And watched the still smiling moon
Wave goodbye from far off in the west!

Dreamland

I live my life among my dreams.
Right or wrong? I cannot say.

It's a land of gentle whimsy,
A place to hide away.

It's a refuge from the storms outside,
Safe and warm and dry.

It's a place to try new things
And no one asks you "why."

They only smile and nod -
They've been down that path themselves

Where their talents and their vision
Were never used, left high up on the shelves.

So enter in this land of dreams,
Though the cost be very high -

A lifetime bound together,
Sharing every sigh.

iry and Flamingoes, Wilcoxen Gardens, Altus OK   Photo by E. Wilcoxen

Saturday Walk

I left my love a sleeping,
And went out for a walk.
I left my love a sleeping,
Went to be renewed by nature's spark,

To restore the eyes that had been dimmed
By all this life's old strife,
To fill them up with all that I could see,
With wonderment and light.

I went out for a walk today;
I went down by the creek,
And as I owe no man my time,
I was free to seek -

Free to look, and listen -
To heed to Nature's call -
Free to spend my time
Just breathing in the wonder of it all!

Through the grassy dew I wandered,
Soaking shoes and socks,
Grass springing soft there underfoot,
Occasionally a rock.

The butterflies on painted wings
Rose up all around.
There, hidden in the grass,
the desert marigolds abound.

The bindweed bloomed in pink and white,
Still the farmer's bane,
But here to this city field
It quite unbidden came.

No one is complaining,
No one knows it's here.
Quietly it spreads out its tendrils
As it reaches far and near.

At the end of this long unbroken field
I saw that the creek was there.
Gentle breezes came to play
And tousled up my hair.

The cottontails froze by the edge
As if I could not see
Who and what they were
If they did not move for me.

But, as I approached them,
As I wandered near,
Suddenly they bolted for cover,
Moving swift in fear.

Just overhead I heard honking
As the geese came flying past.
Not far ahead they settled,
Looking for bugs in the morning grass.

The salt cedar's slender branches
Were hung in green and pink.
Where the water deepened under shadow,
Its surface black as ink,

I saw a turtle sunning,
Soaking up the rays,
Gathering his energy
To greet the coming day.

Down in the bulrushes
A familiar sound was heard.
The croaking of the bullfrog
Seemed to fill the woods.

"Harrumpph," he croaked,
"Harrumpph." I heard him very clear.
He said, "Thank you for visiting -
Now go! 'Cause I live here!"

High overhead, cottonwood branches
Reached out to the sky.
Up in their overarching limbs
I heard the doves and grackles cry.

Further down, near the ground,
The blackbird sang his song,
Said, "Thank you for coming,
Now please move along!"

The sunflowers, in great profusion,
Turned their yellow heads
To worship at the fiery ball
That through the heavens threads.

At last, rounding a gentle curve,
The lake lay on before,
But since we use its water,
We call it "reservoir".

The surface was still shiny smooth
As the newborn sun hung low.
Sparkling diamonds cast their glow
Where ere the gentle breezes go.

Beneath this silky surface,
The dimples would arise,
As fish rose up to dine
On the newly hatching flies.

The cricket sound surrounded.
It pervaded all the world.
"See if you can drink it in!"
Their noisy challenge hurled.

I eagerly accepted,
Raised my eyes up to the sky,
Replenishing my soul
With each moment passing by.

As I filled my well of life, I laughed -
I laughed there right out loud!
Lifting my eyes to heaven,
My gaze devoured the clouds.

"Well done, crickets!"
I heard myself to say,
"Well and truly have we met
The birth of this new day!

But now I must be off -
I must be on my way!
For there is still much to see -
I'm sorry, but I cannot stay!"

So, slipping across a wooden bridge,
I slowly left the stream behind,
On to other paths and pleasures,
To see what I could find -

Past Imagination Station,
Where the happy children play,
Past the roads and alleys
Where the weeds still hold their sway,

Till at last my gate approaches,
My circle is complete.
I enter in the garden walls,
And take a quiet seat.

I think back on my walk today,
An easy morning spent -
Walking, looking, enjoying
All the quiet treasures sent.

Softly I give thanks
For nature's healing way.
I could not think of anything more fine
To start my Saturday!

Path to the roses, Wilcoxen Gardens, Altus OK   Photo by E. Wilcoxen

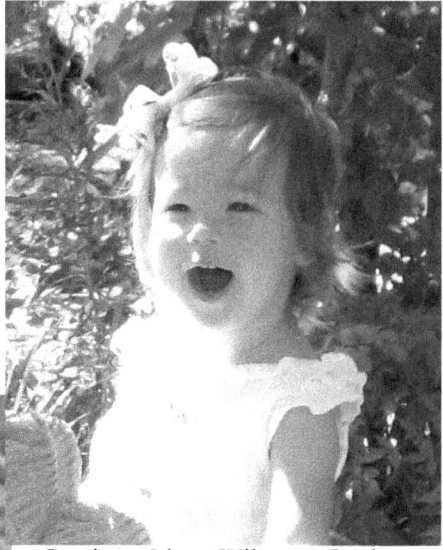

Gracie on Lion, Wilcoxen Gardens

Anthony   Photo by Leslie Brown

Babies Laughing

Babies laughing! Worlds collide!
Babies laughing, they do not try to hide

The bubbling mirth
That shakes their tiny girth

With the all encompassing joy
Of each little girl and each little boy!

It's light dancing just the right way,
Or the perfect toy of play.

It's the taste of something new,
Or something funny that you do.

Babies laughing! Elixir of the age.
Babies laughing! It can turn the very page

Back to innocence and sunshine -
Back to the beginning of our time,

When everything was fresh and new,
And there was everything to do.

The world had not skewed our view,
We could join in soulful laughter too.

Babies laughing! It's a wondrous day!
Babies laughing! To show us the way!

Legs are kicking, arms are flailing,
Eyes bright, mouth open wide unfailing.

It's laughter with whole heart and soul -
Not one thought of holding back, oh, no!

When baby laughs, the world's complete.
No other sound is quite so sweet!

Curved Bridge, Wilcoxen Gardens, Altus OK   Photo by E. Wilcoxen

The Bridge

Somehow the bridge is broken
That connects your heart to mine.

The taste of love's grown bitter,
Left too long out on the vine.

The way has gone untended
That leads from me to you.

Watered now by only tears -
Not garden fair, but weeds to view.

I stare across the broken span
As I long for gentle touch,

Hoping that you, too, wish to stand
Above love's flowing rush.

If one wish I could be granted,
If one wish were mine to make,

I'd stand upon that bridge once more.
I would not make the same mistake.

King of Nothing

I am a King, he cried,
I rule this wide domain.
I am the King of Nothing,
Where no one ever came.

No one can dispute my claim,
For no one else is there.
In all of this nothingness
There is no one else to share.

How did I come to be
the Royal figure here?
Why, there was no one else -
They were all too full of fear!

They pulled away from loneliness.
They chafed at being one.
They all wanted someone else,
And thus they were undone!

Only I could pass the test.
Only I remain!
Only I inhabit
This empty, vast domain.

I am the King of Nothing,
With nothing left inside.
A King stripped bare of all that was -
There's nothing now to hide.

I sit upon my throne alone,
And watch the teardrops fall.
I am the King of Nothing!
There's nothing here at all!

Eternal Moment

The stars are spilled across the heavens,
Like gems on a velvet cloth,
And the moonlight haunts the meadow
On the wings of the dancing moth.

I see the water sparkle,
Ripples shining in the light.
I feel the deep enchantment
Of the magic of the night.
Then I caress you and I kiss you,
As I press your body tight.

Suddenly the world stops spinning!
Time is brought to bay!
This one single moment
Is long as passing day.

The angels sigh above us.
They envy our great love.
They long to share this taste
Of sweetness from above!

As we fall together gently,
Entwined within the night,
I know this is a moment
I'll remember all my life.

The stars are spilled across the heavens,
Like gems on a velvet cloth,
And the moonlight haunts the meadow
On the wings of the dancing moth.

Journey

How many hearts have broken,
How many tears have fallen?
Yet that old siren Love
Still keeps right on a callin'.

From high atop a rocky shore,
She sings her lovely song,
To all the young and innocent,
Who don't know the lyric's wrong.

Fantasies she weaves of a handsome prince,
Or a queen who's ever perfect.
Skillfully, she tells of eternal happiness,
With only harmony, free of any defect.

It's a man who can read her mind.
It's a woman sacrificing all.
He is strong each and every day;
She's waiting at his beck and call,

While above it all, the Angels sing -
They serenade with a golden harp.
Everything is beautiful, and wonderful;
Not one corner is left sharp.

That is the siren's song,
Calling out to innocent young lovers,
So that unthinking, unheeding,
Unaware of the spell they're under

They crash upon the rocks of love,
Sharp obstacles hidden in the sea -
Shipwrecked and torn apart
By the real demands of melding you and me.

Heed not the reckless siren's call!
Do not expect perfection.
You can sail safely free
Only with effort and affection.

You will see that rough or smooth,
This is a joining of the soul.
It travels to such wondrous lands,
That the kings desire to go!

But all their coin cannot
Book them passage here.
Only hearts entwined can enter,
And journey through the years!

Pretty in Pink

Sometimes she's a real go-getter,
Sometimes she's all satin and lace.

Sometimes she's in a hurry.
Sometimes she prefers a slower pace!

Sometimes she talks kind of tough,
Sometimes she'll tell you what she thinks.

Sometimes she's a little bit pushy,
But she's always pretty in pink!

Yes, she's always pretty in pink,
And she lights her face with a smile.

She'll scatter a wee bit of sunshine
To brighten the long weary miles.

She's all about helping somebody -
All about making things right.

She pours her heart out all day long,
Then hurries home at night,

Where she's still up and doing -
She'll cook, and wash, and clean.

And encouragement is all she needs,
The slightest bit will make her beam.

So I do my part with a smile and a wink,
And I tell her she sure does look pretty in pink!

Gypsy Rhythm

Tonight the moon is a silver bowl,
Spilling golden light across the land.

Low in the western sky, as the night rolls by,
Far off a gypsy band

Strum guitars, click their castanets
And dance the gypsy's dance!

As the golden light spills down,
They embrace this one chance.

Let me, too, be wise enough
To seize as my own, this night!

I hear the gypsy rhythm,
And dance my way into the light!

The French Rambler Path, Wilcoxen Gardens   Photo by E. Wilcoxen

Watery Romance

Down the river in a little canoe
Floated Missy Mouse and the Mole.

She said, "This is such a lovely run,"
He said, "I much prefer my hole!"

"Oh, please do show some romance
Down in your cold, cold heart!

I trust you'll play the ukulele gaily,
Come on and do your part!"

"Oh, all right!" he darkly muttered,
"Still, I wish this was another!"

Yet so light and quick his fingers played,
She with kisses him did smother

Till both forgot to steer the canoe,
And as you know without a doubt,

The canoe ran into a great big log,
And quickly tipped them out!

Now, down the river, without a canoe,
Floated Missy Mouse and the mole.

She said, "Sometimes I like to swim!"
He said, "I sure do miss my hole!"

Goldfish and Koi, Wilcoxen Gardens, Altus OK   Photo by E. Wilcoxen

Star Crossed Lovers

Star-crossed lovers, never meant to be,
But the star-crossed lovers couldn't seem to see!

His love was true but short sighted,
Her love was blind - she thought him beknighted.

They pledged their troth, swore that they'd be true,
And I'm sure they meant to, too!

But times got hard, his eye would stray.
She wondered how he ever even came her way.

They built upon the sand, not on the solid rock.
They barely knew each other, and time it seems to mock;

To curse their vows of love, their promises of faith.
For better or worse, sure, but this is more than they can tak

So the star-crossed lovers move along -
Different partners, same old song -

Always searching for the easy way.
Star-crossed lovers they will stay!

For a Mother With Dying Child

Life is not measured by the count of days,
Nor numbered steps along the path.
Who can count the joy
Of children when they laugh?

Though the hours be short
And sadly brief,
Memory of pleasures shared
Is always ours to keep.

Mourn not for young hearts,
Beating cadence to the grave.
Rejoice for the sweetness of our time.
Hold tight to all the gifts they gave -

Laughter, love, and understanding,
Wisdom far beyond their years.
Let them succor you in need.
Let them dry your tears,

So that hand in hand together,
You can walk the shortened way.
Then, when you stand alone at last,
Though hearts will grieve for yesterday,

You will know the beauty.
You will know the gift.
You will remember always
All the love your child could give!

Warm Winter Day

A warm day in winter is like
Flowers from the bower.
Sunshine in the dreary months -
What a welcome, warming shower!

Today was sunny, bright, and warm,
A potion for the soul.
I sat beneath a leafless tree,
And soaked in the warming glow.

A warm day in winter is like
A hug from a loving child.
I sat beneath a tree today,
Felt the sun's embrace, and smiled!

Stop Time

They say that time
  ...Stops...
For no man,

But moments of heartbreak
Come as close as you can.

There is eternity
In the tear that falls.

Nothing counts before or after -
Nothing matters much at all!

Water Lilies and Irises, Wilcoxen Gardens, Altus OK   Photo by E. Wilcoxen

Water Lilies

The blossoms float upon the surface
Or stand and softly sway

In the colors of the palette -
Red, blue, yellow, and more there on display.

Bright petals beckon dragonflies.
They come in flights galore.

There are soft green pads for landing,
Fragrance for the bees, and more.

Yet underneath the splendor,
Hidden, unseen by anyone,

Lay roots both long and deep.
That's where the work is done.

It's like a love that flowers -
So much of that is hidden too.

Unseen by all the outside world,
But precious beyond jewels -
       the roots of me and you.

Thirty Years

To me the years are not hourglass grains,
They are more like water in a glass.
So I was quite surprised, my dear,
To learn that thirty years have passed!

I would not have thought it,
So quickly they have sped.
Thirty years!
And still you warm my bed –

And my soul!
You are a comfort and a friend,
For thirty years,
Yet, I think that you have always been –

That somehow this was fated –
Too much for mortal man.
Somewhere the Gods were smiling,
And lent a gentle hand -

Just a quiet push
To bring two people close,
To live their lives in greater joy
Than I could ever hope.

Thirty years!
Thank you love, and thanks again,
For all the sweetness, all the joy,
For everything within.

Remember dear,
this glass is not yet drained.
Let's try for thirty more,
and then do it all again!

Silent House

There is a silent house,
Hidden in the woods.
It tells a lonely story
Through the changing seasons' moods.

Stark and bare
In winter's quiet keep,
It shakes in the wind,
Flanked by white snows deep.

Sadly sitting brown and bare
As Spring wakes up the land -
In the midst of green and growth,
It lifts an empty hand.

'Midst Summer's splendor,
It sits in melancholy -
The contrast of life and not
A portrait of our folly.

The hollow frame just watches
As autumn colors shine in gold and red,
Dreaming of the glory that once was
Before happy people fled.

Eerie in the moonlight,
The shadows come to play.
In the silent house
Only memories hold sway.

Yesterday Is Gone

Today has become tomorrow
And yesterday is gone.
If I knew where time goes,
I'd tell it in a song!

Your love was sweet,
Like some romantic line.
But as they say in fairy tales,
That was once upon a time!

Today your love is cold,
For us no tomorrow comes.
The clock is tolling midnight,
But the future is struck dumb!

It's the end of a day,
It's the end of our love.
It's the end of our time,
Together hand in glove.

Today has become tomorrow,
And yesterday is gone!
If I just knew how, I'd turn back time
To before it all went wrong!

Speak the Words That Bind

Speak the words, and seal the bond,
Say "I DO," forever's magic wand.

Now it's always together,
Hand in hand the tether

To keep you ever close,
Amidst the spinning cosmos!

Like the words of a childhood tale,
Where heroes always win and never fail-

From eyes that see only the sparkles of the day-
Start happy tears as Daddy gives you away.

Another claims your heart and speaks the words,
So nervous that he can scarce be heard.

"I now pronounce" - you float back down the aisle.
Reality is for another time – this is the day of smiles!

Heart of Hearts

Where do you hide your heart of hearts,
That tender, tender part?
Do you ever let it see the light of day,
Or does it labor in the dark?

Why not take it out today,
and share it with another –
Open wide the window,
Let the sun shine with your lover.

Freed from old perception,
Let your heart of hearts rejoice!
You'll feel the warming tingle
Rewarding love's true choice.

There is a lightness in the soul,
Joy beyond imagining,
A newness to the world,
Now filled with wondrous things!

Your heart will grow wings,
Like the angels up above.
You'll fly away in dreams,
held aloft by love.

Forget the hide - go seek!
Let your heart of hearts come out to play.
Release him from his dungeon
And everything will change today!

One More

One more dawn,
One more morning's glory,

One more sunset
Before the end of story.

One more moment,
Enraptured by your love,

One more evening
With sparkling stars above.

One more time,
Your hand in mine,

One more eternity
In which our hearts entwine!

One more is all I ask.
One more, one more, I plead.

One more for now and always -
One more is all I need!

Wild Lands

Wild lands await beyond, beyond,
Beyond this tiny place.

Hand in hand, and heart to heart,
Let us join the wider chase.

Through the cathedrals of old Europe
To the ancient China land

We will gaze in enraptured wonder -
Ours the world to span!

From sounding seas to mountains -
From deserts to forest green -

We will wander two together,
Past wonders seldom seen!

Wild lands await, my dear.
The road begins outside.

Come with me. Please, come with me,
Let's start our carpet ride.

The first step is the hardest -
Each footfall smoother then.

Come walk the wild world, darling.
Our chance may never come again.

Chinese Guardian Lion, Wilcoxen Gardens, Altus OK   Photo by E. Wilcoxen

Love in the Water

Silver waters flow around our bodies
Like islands in the sea.
As we come together in the cool wet,
I hold you tight to me!

Moonlight falls softly,
Reflecting off your soft, wet skin.
Universes collide as lips touch,
And ancient feelings rise again!

Nothing in all the vast world matters -
Flesh seeks after flesh;
Standing outside of time,
The old is ever fresh!

Passions roar, passions roar,
Take me home!
Rhythm of love, rhythm of love,
We belong to you alone!

The rising crescendo explodes
Into a pleasure so deep,
So rich, that it is the place
We seek and seek.

In love's afterglow we sigh, contented.
The truth has been revealed -
That in all the endless worlds on worlds
There is nothing more precious.
We have heard the bells of angels peal!

While it is true that
"The unexamined life is not worth living,"
I contend the over examined life is not worth having!
...............Eddie D. Wilcoxen

Because It's There

I read today that science in its knowledge quest
Now knows why it is that we all have sex.

They said there were exactly 237 reasons.
And that's just basic – doesn't count the teasin'!

This is not more or less -
It's exactly 237 reasons for sex.
Write them a letter, they'll send you the specs.

There are exactly 237 –
Those are the reasons for going to heaven!

But any fool knows why bare humans pair.
We all have sex just because it's there!

Hearts on Fire

Hearts on fire,
Beating desire,
Hand in hand we go!

Soul to soul,
Two one whole,
This one thing we know-

That together we will stay
Through all the coming days.
Lost in love's rhythm,

With hearts on fire,
Beating desire,
Grateful for all we've been given!

Summer Years

Summer years of bright sunshine gone,
Time less warm, wrapped in autumn, lingers on.

Winter's chill is not far away.
Still, we're together blessing the day

That fate and the very stars above
In perfect alignment proclaimed our love.

Hand in hand, we walk through the many years-
You to calm my worries, me to dry your tears.

Now that the end is closer than the start,
Sometimes I wonder about my heart.

On that coming day when left alone -
In that time when you won't be coming home,

Will I remember the good, and persevere,
Or be lost, immobilized, just sitting here,

Remembering summer days of sunshine.

Goodbye

Memories, like dried bones,
Rattle in my mind -
The refuse of another time,
Back when love was blind.

Memory, bone marrow broken,
Meaning scraped away,
Left cold and hard and dry -
Bereft of warmth. Empty thoughts of yesterday!

Those times of love together,
The special ones we knew -
I now know were only lies.
I need no illusion to see me through.

I recall it all.
I see it now so clear,
Your love an act,
Like machinations from King Lear.

Beneath your smile,
A cold, cold sneer.
I could not see it sooner,
Blinded by a tear.

But my recollection's strong now,
The truth has set me free!
Those dry bones merely dust now,
Something less than memory.

Tears, Dew, and Broken Glass

The diamond dew glistens
On the waiting morning grass,
Like sparkling tears
Through brilliant sunlit shafts.

She won't be back;
This road runs out of sight.
It's carried her far, far away,
Into the waiting night.

As the blackness swallowed
The red retreating lights,
There came the chill awareness
That it will never more be right.

Rocking in silence through long cold hours
No answers were in sight.
The room grew crowded with
What if, could have, should have, and I might.

Off down the road, I see deceptive glitter
In the dawning – this day is broken.
Those shining shards are worth about as much
as all the promises and true love tokens.

Tears, dew, and broken glass –
The diamonds of a fool .
Like love's illusions, they shine so bright -
Just imitation jewels!

Laughing Moonbeam

I held a moonbeam in my hand,
It laughed and giggled there,
Then silently shattered into silver slivers
That seemed to dash off everywhere!

It had slipped into my room
By my bedroom window,
And bade me look into the sky
To see the rising moon glow.

So I did, and moonbeam sisters
Poured down all around,
Leaving me, too, laughing and giggling
As they danced across the ground!

Nodding Off

The land of Nod is calling;
It beckons to the sleepy head,
Says, "Sail away, away with me,
Away with me to bed.

"Together we will see distant shores,
Earth's treasures we'll explore.
A night of magic awaits in Nod,
Where mighty rivers roar!

"We'll dance among the fairies,
We'll climb upon the stars,
Drink from the heavens' dipper,
Travel, oh, so far.

"We will spend the night together
In this wondrous land called Nod.
Mighty deeds transpire here –
We'll touch the hand of God!

"Then at the end of night,
I'll bring you safely home,
To live amongst the day folk,
'Til darkness bids you roam!"

Lifetime Love

Secret things
And private dreams -
Joy behind a door!

The years go by,
Yet passion thrives,
And leaves us wanting more.

I hear lament
Of love that's spent -
Grown old, and hard, and cold.

Yet ours feels new,
And special, too -
Free, not bought or sold.

So, softly dear,
The time is near
To shut the world away.

Behind the blind,
Sweet the find,
Where passion holds its sway!

Brugmansia "Angel Trumpets"   Photo by E. Wilcoxen

Angel Trumpets

Sweet delight,
Like island spice,
Angel trumpets in the night.

Deliciously soft,
The fragrance wafts aloft,
Like butterflies in flight.

Exotic scent,
Heaven sent,
Angel trumpets in the night!

This House That We Two Fill

I'm awake and ambling about the house
In the middle of the night.
I just shut the bedroom door
Where Joan is sleeping tight.

I put aside my writing,
Make myself a cup of tea.
Wandering to the moonlit window,
I take a sip, as it occurs to me,

That we two fill this house,
Despite its rambling rooms.
Just the two of us
Make it grow and bloom!

When I shut that bedroom door,
I heard a gentle snoring.
I just had to chuckle -
That woman's anything but boring.

She's an energizer bunny,
Even in her sleep.
She can't just lie there quiet;
She must be counting sheep,

Or helping someone out,
Maybe looking after me.
Through the years I've come to count on that,
But that won't always be.

Two of us fill this house,
All two stories tall.
Someday it will be just one of us
Wandering down this hall.

That thought hit me hard tonight,
I really don't know why.
Maybe it's the passing years-
They're starting to pile high.

The two of us fill this house,
Every board and beam.
One of us alone here –
How different that must seem!

I wonder if the love we've shared,
All the memories made,
Can fill the empty space that's left
By the turning of the spade.

Ashes to ashes, dust to dust,
Time just rolls along,
Years will beget the decades,
'Til one of us is gone.

Cup in hand, quietly I stand
At the bedroom door.
Silently I watch her sleep,
No more gentle snore,

Just the rise and fall of breathing,
Amidst the crumpled covers,
That brings to mind the many times
We rolled together here as lovers.

I look around at this life we've found,
In this house that we two fill,
And I realize that as long as one remains,
So, too, the other will.

A life cannot run forever
Like a river to the sea.
It has its start. It has its finish -
For you, for her, for me,

So live it well,
And fear be damned!
Gently I touch her hand,
Shut the door, then for a moment stand,

As I think about this house
That we have filled so well.
I have to laugh because
Here some part of us will always dwell -

In the haunted house, where the spirits sing,
And tend the flowers in the Spring.
Where shadowy specters sit at the swing
And chronicle the joy it brings.

Still night air,
Yet there's a gentle breeze upon the stair.
Curtains sway and laughter, far away, is heard,
Though no one's really there.

It's only ghosts in the moonlight,
Providing a thrill,
As we wander contented, room to room,
In this house that we two fill!

Entry of Wilcoxen Gardens, Altus OK   Photo by E. Wilcoxen

A Poet's Heart

A poet's heart, a poet's heart,
It beats within my chest,
Sounding out, pounding out,
These hours I love the best.

With book in hand, I make my stand
With sages from the past,
Thus, word by word, I have heard
Immortal thoughts that last.

Wielding words, shielding words,
The poet's weapons flash!
They cut away the petty play -
Deep into emotions slash!

Speak of love, speak of love -
The poet sinks his pen
Down into flesh - blood so fresh,
Springs from where emotion's been.

Or shed a tear for one so dear,
Who walks this earth no more.
Somewhere a poet's written the lines
To open wide that door

So that teardrops fall. Teardrops fall
And cleanse the very soul,
With a rushing tide, a river's ride,
That leaves you fresh and whole.

Sometimes in fancy,
Mind lightly dancing, I dream in fairy dust,
Or hear the beat of trampling feet,
Watch history turn to rust.

Where ere I go,
I always know a poet's gentle hand.
This way's been trod,
Long and hard, by many a better man -

Who called himself -
Who knew himself - a poet in his heart,
Who knows the way for feet of clay,
And shows me where to start!

The Last Rose

The last rose has faded...

The nights are growing cold,
Fading picture, tarnished gold,
It's a story worn and old.

The last rose has faded...

I still love her,
And I'd tell her,
But there is no more forever.

The last rose has faded...

Now the springtime's done.
Gone the golden days of sun,
The chilly mists have won.

The last rose has faded...

No more sweet embrace,
Love's teasing taste-
It's just too late.

The last rose has faded...

My heart is growing cold,
And memory cannot hold -
Time is just too bold.

The last rose has faded...

One More Time

He said, "Let's try it one more time."
What a worn out, tired old line.

It never does come out right -
Again you're crying in the night.

Try it one more time,
Go on, listen to his line,

And you'll be forever chained
To a man who just won't change.

What one more really means
Is an endless run of drama scenes -

Accusations, fights and lies,
Half baked stories, alibis.

One more time is just too much,
And as you recoil from his touch

Suddenly you realize -
Standing there in complete surprise -

That one more time has come and gone.
Time is up! You're moving on!

The Wheel

Ever moving, never still -
The wheel of life must turn.

As my hungry heart keeps beating -
Always for love it yearns!

Wheel of life, wheel of life,
Throw some luck my way!

Eternal, cold, unspeaking -
Still, I know it's in your sway.

You can do this one thing for me.
You control the cosmic dice.

Someone to love, someone to hold,
Only this and nothing else suffice.

Upon the wheel I'm spinning.
I face the world alone.

Upon the wheel comes knowing -
It takes two to make a home.

Redwood Wheel, Wilcoxen Gardens, Altus OK   Photo by E. Wilcoxen

Smile to Tear

Between the first small smile
And the final salty tear
Lies the time that is your life.

All the days of happiness,
All the nights of passion,
All the anger, all the strife

Fill this one small moment
Between eternities -
From nothing into void.

It's one quick breath,
So breath deep
And just enjoy!

Small and mighty,
Each shall see this one brief time
Upon the globe.

So, live it, love it, devour it -
The fire of life
Will soon grow cold.

Roses Everywhere

Roses arch above the gate,
Roses near the pond,
Roses in the garden,
They just go on and on!

Roses everywhere!

Delicate and delicious,
Their scent is in the air,
Erasing doubt and worry,
Removing weary care,

Roses everywhere!

Red and yellow, gold and pink,
Their varied palettes shine.
Soft blush petals glow in the sun,
Casting a spell divine.

Roses everywhere!

Roses in your hair,
Reflected by your eyes.
Roses all around us
As my heart so gently sighs!

Roses everywhere!

Eyes of Love

They say the eyes of love are blind -
I beg to differ.
Far from being blind,
There's a special sight that love offers -

The ability to see past flaws,
All the way to the heart.
It's vision into the future -
You know you'll never part.

The eyes of love see possibilities -
What could come to be.
It may not happen,
But just the chance can set you free.

It looses the soul to soar,
And the heart to hope.
No, the eyes of love are not blind.
They simply see a longer slope!

Matches and Gasoline

MATCHES and GASOLINE.
Flames abound!
Just me and her,
No one else around!

It' ain't love,
That's a sure thing,
But it's HOT!
Like burning gasoline.

No spark needed,
The FIRE leaps high.
Here alone together,
Our first try.

Fumbling fingers
And hurried FLESH.
First time,
Not necessarily best.

But it BURNS,
Down deep, in your teens,
And you never forget
MATCHES and GASOLINE!

Johnny and June

Johnny, the wild black haired boy,
Loved June, of Carter family fame.
Johnny, with big voice and guitar,
Was making himself a name.

Money, women, temptations all,
Flowed like the riches of kings.
But, alone with his thoughts,
In the quiet night, he wanted just one thing.

The man in black was smitten.
June had won his heart.
He'd take her hand and marry -
They'd make a brand new start!

June felt the pull of fate,
And she already knew-
There may not be just one soul mate,
But they are far and few.

So Johnny and June were wed,
Lived and loved for many years.
They left us a legacy of hope,
Two hearts as one, fighting past the fears.

Standing in the ring of fire,
Holding the world at bay,
They sang their song so sweetly -
I hear it still today!

Bank on It

A gentle hand upon the shoulder,
A simple word of praise,
Warm lovers embrace, or mother's hug,
These are the things that make our days.

It's not the endless chatter
From that box up on the wall.
You don't need second hand emotions.
I promise you, you still have them all.

So head out into the world
With eyes that truly see.
Share some human emotion!
Let's see who you can be!

Depart with happy heart,
And smile a caring smile.
Help someone get on a bus,
Carry groceries down an aisle.

Share a kind look,
Give a word of thanks.
You'll find more value there
Than in all the world's rich banks!

Heartbeat

Hearts... beat... in... the night,
Counting out our days.

Hearts... beat... in... the night,
Like the pounding of the waves.

Hearts... beat... in... the night,
Sure as the sun above.

Hearts... beat... in... the night,
The rhythm of our love!

Confusion

She hungers for the words -
He resists.

She tells of her need,
She insists.

He bucks up hard -
Spits the bit.

Men and women in love,
How confused can you get?

This House Was Built With Love

This house was built with love.
The angels blessed it from above.

They surveyed it all with pride,
With contentment deep inside,
For they knew, and not surmised,

This house was built with love.

Inside, enjoy a cozy fire,
Blessed by brick, rising ever higher,

To warm the body and the soul,
Spur contemplation of life's goal.
Safe and warm - an ember's glow -

This house was built with love.

The furniture's not new.
Years, it's seen a few,

But it's comfy and it's clean,
And the atmosphere's serene.
Come on in, you'll see what I mean.

This house was built with love.

Let's go gather in the kitchen.
Did I even mention -

It's the biggest room that's here,
The place to sip that cup of cheer -
They come to visit far and near.

This house was built with love.

Outside in the garden
We can sit and talk, or wander

Past waterfalls and ponds,
Along paths that ramble on
As birds sweetly sing their song.

This house was built with love.

Love has infused its very being,
From hardwood floor to ceiling,

From stained glass lamp and windows,
To the covering of the pillows,
Love just rolls, and flows, and billows.

This house that was built with love.

This house was built with love,
And like a hand inside a glove

It suits us perfectly -
We're happy, can't you see,
To be living two as "we"

In this house we built with love.

River of Time

Time is like a river,
Ever flowing to the sea,
And you and I are drifting
Through this landscape that we see.

It's the ever changing story,
Yet always it's the same.
Days come and go, and turn to years,
And no one is to blame.

We're all refugees adrift -
On our way to God knows where,
Clinging tight against the night,
Our shivering souls stripped bare.

Sometimes we get it right,
Often it goes awry.
Despite our love, we disagree -
I can't tell you why.

Yet, there is something I can say to you,
And too often I don't bother.
That is "I love you,"
And know that we can go on farther.

We can travel to the end of time,
As for us it is ordained.
We'll ride the tide together
Through toil, and strife, and pain.

We'll sail into the sunshine
That awaits on distant shore.
Hand in hand, we'll sight the land,
And explore forever more!

Mountain Waterfall, Wilcoxen Gardens Photo by E. Wilcoxen

Sound of Lonely

In the stillness, not a sound-
It's almost like a weight.

The silence echoes your goodbye.
It's a thought I've grown to hate.

Silence - it's the sound of leaving,
Yet you can hear my old heart break,

As lonely tears drop to the floor,
Shattering illusions I tried so hard to make.

Goodbye in silence, goodbye in the night -
Now where the hell's my drink?

I'll be all right, I tell myself -
That's what I say, not what I really think.

In the sadness, not a sound -
Just the echo of second thoughts, if onlys.

It's stillness filled with sorrow...
And the growing sound of lonely.

Walks in Beauty

She walks in beauty like the day,
Radiance so bright the stars must hide away,
And the moon fear to show his face,
For want of fading in the glow of her reflected grace.

A celestial being bound to earth -
More than golden treasures worth!
Her countenance and presence shine
To fill love's cup, like flowing wine.

Gracefully she moves, like the sun across the sky,
Her glowing step the focus of each and every eye.
Light and lithe she moves, like a gentle stirring breeze,
Awakening each heart she meets with unselfconscious ease.

Her hair flows down in flaxen curls around her china face,
Making all who glance her way forgetful of all things base.
Her shining eyes look outward and challenge all the world,
Daring them to keep apace, to accept the gauntlet hurled.

There is a majesty in the strength of her demeanor,
An appreciation of strong resolve by all who've ever seen her.
Yet there is a gentleness, a sweetness that surrounds.
Where she in beauty walks, love surely must abound!

Dancing in Love

Cheek to cheek,
Dancing in the night,
Heart to heart,
The feeling's oh, so right!

Eye to eye,
As love's old feelings rise.
Body to body,
Holding back the sighs.

Beat to beat,
The music does enrapture.
Moment to moment,
Surely we are captured!

Bound in love's spell,
The world spins slow,
And we are incredulous
When told it's time to go.

Rose Petal Dreams

The first blush of love
Is like the sweet scent of a rose.
It feels like forever, blooming full and fine.
Then suddenly, before reason even knows

The petals fall away, each one soft in its blush,
No longer a coherent whole –
Just bits and pieces of all that was –
Ah, but that's the way it goes!

It's rose petal dreams,
And love's memories of sweet days,
By lovers long abandoned -
Now gone their separate ways,

Yet remembering still the newness
In that first blush of Spring -
When love was red, and blooming full –
When love was everything,

Before the petals fell away
To reveal this emptiness.
Now rose petal dreams -
That's all that's left of us!

Cozy Fire

Tonight I sit beside a cozy fire
And watch the dancing flames.

I think of roads I've travelled,
Of the changes time has made.

The dreams of youth so far away
It's hard to say for sure,

Still, I think this moment, this right now,
Is not far from what they were.

The crackle of the blazing logs...
My love is close at hand...

Tonight I sit by a cozy fire,
And I am a happy man!

For Joan

I need an ear to hear, someone to share,
Else the thoughts will not come out.
So I write, and Joan listens and comforts me,
Protects me from the doubt.

From behind my wall of armor
Soft emotions bubble through.
Then I sift them, and I shape them,
So I can share them all with you!

But without that outer fortress,
It would all be just too close.
It would overwhelm in sadness,
Or be lost in braggart's boast.

So thank you for this center,
This protected quiet place,
From which I venture out in safety,
Knowing shelter when I just can't stand the pace.

Precious

Wizened eyes and weathered hands,

Years fly by.

Friends come, and friends go.

Friends die.

And the few that remain are precious.

Dreamers

This enchanted ship of dreams
Sails a velvet sky!
Hand in hand, we ride the wind
As time goes rushing by.

The world turns, bringing days and nights,
Then more.
Together we stand upon the bow,
Facing the future's roar,

Knowing that we will stand
Or fall as one -
That these winds of change
Will not find us undone.

With love flying as our banner,
To the precipice we sail,
Where mounting high on eagle wings
We'll rend the heaven's veil!

Love's Design

Love hears the softest whisper.
Love knows the gentlest touch.

Guard close and hard those angry words
Lest they become too much.

Soft and supple is the fabric of your togetherness.
It is woven out of trust.

Don't thoughtlessly break the threads -
Breathe deep, and then just hush!

Too many irritations, too much said aloud,
Will disturb the pattern's plan.

Make your design a thing of beauty -
The look of love between a woman and a man.

Where Is My Love

"Where is my love?"
She is not here.

"Where is my love?
I long to hold her near."

"Where is my love?
Where has she gone?"

"Where is my love?
Will she be staying long?"

"Where is my love?"
I ask the frozen ground

"Where is my love?"
It echoes… and not another sound!

Come Away With Me

Leave the dusty memory and those who cannot see,
My love, and come away with me.
Let the briny deep it's long held secrets keep,
And come away with me!

Let the clouds go by in an endless sky,
And come away with me.
Ashes to ashes, dust to dust - 'twill always be enough.
'Tis time, my love, to come away with me.

Leave the raging sea, you were meant for me,
And I will love you true.
They have had their say, must live life their own way,
As I will live for you.

My love, come away,
Come away with me.

The storm approaches, I hear echoing reproaches.
I see you lost and torn.
Let your heart be your guide, come away my bride.
Let our love be born!

Come away my love, away my love,
Come away with me!

If I Could Write

If I could write a way to fly,
I'd take this pen and climb the sky!

If I could write a growing flower,
This page would be a rosy bower.

If I could write the stars and moon,
I'd save them for a night in June.

If I could only write a cloud,
I'd laugh and chuckle right out loud.

If I could write for us a song,
I'd ask for you to sing along.

If I could write the shining sun,
This page with glory would be done.

If I could write the rainbow's end,
We'd have a treasure we could spend.

If I could write a living dream,
We'd dance on air in sunlit beams.

If I could write a growing tree,
The shade would envelope you and me.

If I could write the end of time,
I'd have enough to make this rhyme.

And if I could write about true love,
This page would shame the stars above!

Golden Day Lily, Wilcoxen Gardens, Altus OK   Photo by E. Wilcoxen

Sing a Song

Sing a song of passion,
Sing a song of love.
Sing a song as ancient
As the wolf's serenade
To the moon above.

Sing a song of newness,
Of the fresh green spring,
The rising tide of life
Engulfing everything.

Sing a song of quiet,
Sumptuous summer nights,
The gentle tune of cricket chirps,
And starry, starry lights.

Sing a song of autumn,
Colors yellow, orange, and red,
The crush of dry leaves
Sounding where we tread.

Sing a song of winter,
White snow piling high,
Of a walk in a frozen wonderland
Beneath a pale dim sky.

Sing your song to me, my love,
Sing your song to me.
I will listen with bated breath
Upon a trembling knee

For the song that fills completely,
The tune that makes me whole,
The notes that seem to know
The very meat and marrow of my soul!

Sing your song to me, my love,
Sing it all our days!
Though dim and dark the path,
This melody will always stay!

Foolish Heart

Who has not had a foolish heart?
For all hearts are foolish at the start!

They give themselves in gladness, holding nothing back!
They offer love so freely - open, honest, caring -
No deception and no act!

Their innocence is laughable, the sophisticated shout.
They joke about those so naive
In what life and love is all about.

They revel in the knowledge that love is just a game -
Once you've played a time or two
It's all the same old same.

Yet the foolish heart strikes near the mark.
Without guile or plan,
The innocent give up their heart.

Sometimes it is broken. Sometimes it is abused.
But at least they know it's beating!
They know it is in use!

And in plumbing the depths of the human soul,
The foolish heart treads
Where the wise fear to go!

When those of more experience hold back and fear the fall,
The foolish heart leaps with love's abandon -
Perhaps...not foolish... after all!

Texas Star Hibiscus, Wilcoxen Gardens, Altus OK   Photo by E. Wilcoxen

INDEX

INDEX

ABOUT THE AUTHOR

Eddie D. Wilcoxen is a man of many interests and talents. In addition to being a popular storyteller and poet, he has served as Oklahoma Poet Laureate, is a three time national Karate champion, was declared an "Official Olympic Hero" and was chosen to carry the Olympic Torch to Atlanta in 1996.

He is also profiled in Who's Who of American Teachers, hosts a top rated radio show, and has created a personal garden featured in magazines and on television. He and his wife Joan live in Altus, Oklahoma.

Please visit www.eddiestuff.com.

Other Books by Eddie D. Wilcoxen

- Reflections of a Wandering Mind
- Oklahoma Proud!
- Ridin'! Rodeo and Range
- Animal ABC's - A Book of Whimsy
- More Reflections of a Wandering Mind
- Songbook in My Head
- Wounds of War - A Tale of Two Americas
- Everybody Needs Heroes
- Faith, Hope and Poetry
- Christmas Past and Christmas Presents

Please visit our website

www.eddiestuff.com

I have always enjoyed those "hidden tracks" on music albums, so I thought I'd do the same thing poetically. Here is my "hidden poem"

.................Eddie D. Wilcoxen

Encore

Encore my love! Encore! Let's do it all again!
Encore my love! Encore! I'm ready to begin.
Just the thought brings a tingle to my skin,
Stirring up that old time yen.

Encore my love! Encore!

Encore my dear! Encore! Let's start the years anew.
Encore my dear! Encore! Let me spend them all with you.
We could do things even better now,
With our lifetime of love and know how!

Encore my love! Encore!

Encore! Encore! Hear the thunderous ovation!
Encore! Encore! Applause for all the love it's taken.
We beat the odds through the years galore,
But we're still not ready for that distant shore.
Take a bow! Let's do it all once more!

Encore, my love! Encore!

www.ingramcontent.com/pod-product-compliance
Lightning Source LLC
Chambersburg PA
CBHW071139090426
42736CB00012B/2166